There is a marvelous and liberating breadth to the subject matter in this fine collection but a recurring sense that these are the utterances of a heterogenous twenty-first-century soul stuck with Shakespeare on the checkout line of mundane twenty-first-century existence. At one with doing the balancing act that this predicament entails, the poet offers us delightful glimpses out of the conundrum, intimating what it means to be suddenly on the precipice of revelation. The situations range as widely as does the mosaic of modern living—from the workaday to the rarefied but always with the tantalizing potential for a moment of visionary insight, the potential for some searing truth to be found in the graceless contemporary moment. Whether it is rescuing tomatoes in a fallow garden or trapping a mouse in the gingersnaps, trailing an exotic woman in the produce department or standing among teenage judo novices about to demonstrate their mastery of highly disciplined and sublime martial art, we are reminded that, for the attentive and focused in life, we may be "always on the blank tatami (where) a master awaits." This is Julio Marzán's desideratum, his poetry's triumph, and the transcendent intimation he brings to his readers.

George Wallace,
writer in residence at the Walt Whitman Birthplace

Julio Marzán is a poet of intelligence and integrity, an original and independent voice for decades. He is a sharp-eyed observer of the urban world—witness his poems "Jury Duty," focused on the mothers of defendants, and "Subway Crustacean," about a single human being representing the epidemic of homelessness in New York at the time. These poems spring from a deep well of compassion, nowhere better illustrated than by the title poem about a mouse that meets a miserable fate at the hands of the poet, who cannot bear the suffering he has inflicted. We also meet a teacher in these pages, at home with literary allusion yet painfully aware of the struggle to teach those most in need. Julio Marzán has my deepest gratitude and respect.

Martín Espada,
winner of the 2021 National Book Award

The Glue Trap

and Other Poems

by
Julio Marzán

The Glue Trap

Fernwood Press
Newberg, Oregon
www.fernwoodpress.com

Printed in the United States of America

Cover and page design: Mareesa Fawver Moss
Cover photo: Muhammad owsama

ISBN 978-1-59498-100-5

For Silvina

Contents

Acknowledgments

"Cosmic Debate" originally appeared in *Mobius: The Poetry Magazine*, 2009

"David Koresh among the Angels" previously appeared in the anthology *Winged Spirits* (F.D. Reeve, Ed., Calgary: Bayeux Arts, 1992)

"Dumpster Roses" was originally published in *The West Texas Literary Review*, Fall 2018.

"The Glue Trap" was originally published in *Ploughshares*, 2005.

"Jury Duty" was originally published in *The New York Daily News*, 2007.

"Like a Lawyer" was originally published in *The Nassau Review*, 1999.

"New and Improved Detergent" was originally published in *The West Texas Literary Review*, Fall 2018.

"Ode" was originally published in the anthology *Paper Dance* (Persea Books, 1995).

"Poetry D.J." previously appeared in *Tin House, 2002*.

"Reflections in Stalled Traffic" was originally published in *For David Ignatow* (Wesleyan University Press), an anthology honoring David Ignatow's 80th birthday.

"Saving Tomatoes" was originally published in *The Nassau Review*, 2000

"Strong Wind" was originally published in *For New Orleans & Other Poems*, edited by Ashis Gupta, Introduction by F. D. Reeve, (Calgary: Bayeux Arts, 2007).

"Student D" originally appeared in *Mobius: The Poetry Magazine*, 2010.

An earlier version of "Poems of the Freak" was e-published in *A Gathering of the Tribes*, March 2018.

1. Reflections in Stalled Traffic

The Glue Trap

The long-tailed mouse that gnawed
a hemisphere into my box of ginger snaps,
the dust-gray mouse whose dung
speckled the kitchen floor and countertop,
the mold-puff mouse whose claws
rummaged paper garbage bags,
creaking crumpled cellophane,
the pointy-nosed mouse, nostrils trembling,
the defenseless mouse, cute and sad-eyed,
shocked by sudden light,
the chomping, big-footed mouse that evoked
longer-toothed rodent relations,
the heaving, golf-ball fat mouse
expecting to run back to digest,
sleep in his jagged hole in the wall,
has stepped into the glue trap,
spent the night defecating, squirming,
feet stuck, knees unable to unleash,
so it can only rock desperately,
taking dream-lunges into the home
it will never enter again.

This condemned, filth-fuzzy tear,
this handball of breath, whose snout
rested on glue for once and forever,
squeaks in my kitchen cabinet
and now, glued to its dilemma,
I must recall its tiny rolled feces,
the disgust it sowed in my food,

the half-moon signature of its gnaw,
the nightly invasion of its hunger,
forget completely the innocence of its hunger
trapped in my invasion of its life,
deserved to be snuffed out mercifully,
crushed by a mallet or well-poisoned,
or coldly dropped into boiling water
rather than be left suffering for days,
gasping for food and the freedom of swift legs.

But I have no mallet or poison,
nor the stomach to boil it
and smell its cooked odor,
no means to ennoble my animal role:
my paw hurls my shredded prey
deep into buzzing forest
where second by second
its squeak dissolves in the cosmos,
day's wind, night's rustle, and the ancient hunger of insects.

Indelible Lessons

Teen boys lined up in white *guis*—
eyes leveled beams of respect—
kneel warrior-erect, sit
butts on heels, palms on laps,
mirror our Japanese *senseis'*
bows forehead to floor.

Bards of judo those three
blackbelt Kodokan graduates,
limber perfection still judging,
still grading my mastery:
the shoulder-throw Watanabe,
the knee-trip wiz Osuna,
tall, dawn-smile Yamada,
giant whose gentle bare feet
lightingly sweep in my dream dojo.

During *ronduri*, as *kyais* ignited
incandescent my solar plexus,
each demanded: "Giulio, at-tack, at-tack,"
no different woman or man,
fake foot-sweep swiveled
into a hip throw else hook
a knee, slam down then choke,
one seamless act chanting
the kyai's searing lyric of strength.

But clawed ferocity gilded with art,
every trip, sweep, or throw
judged in Japanese accent
to correct rhythm, balance, form. . .
three molten voices still pouring
steel truth that now coaches
match after match against the poem:
be not blithe, assuming, or inflated;
always on the blank *tetami*
for my mastery, a master waits.

New and Improved Detergent

Blood was never a sacred thing.
Read old books; believe the screen.
Red stains now only lightly cling.

One guy covets another's ring.
Bullets riddle one soft spleen.
Blood was never a sacred thing.

Bump a shoulder, insult a king.
He stabs you to impress his queen.
Red stains now only lightly cling.

Quiet that baby, break its wing.
Fat hard pillow dumped unseen.
Blood was never a sacred thing.

My land once one genetic string.
Bombs return how it had been!
Red stains now only lightly cling.

"Thou shalt not" is a bygone thing.
Modernity suds up, leaves us clean.
Blood was never a sacred thing.
Red stains now only lightly cling.

Saving Tomatoes

Parallel vines coil up
taut cords perpendicular
to black, fertile earth.

Vertical musical scales
for fat juicy notes—
green, orange, red—

best played just ripe
not dropped split open,
juice glazing earth.

Perfect fallen ones
I set out to rescue,
one bucket not enough;

but see imperfect ones
differently destined,
if no less deliciously,

to feed other life
writhing underfoot
or chirping overhead.

Into my shadow one
bucket I carry, crushing
ripe and rotting red.

Dumpster Roses

for Silvina

Dozens—mauve, yellow, peach—
gowned in cellophane,
baby's breath lace,
costumed to marry
humans that jilted them,
now overdressed, aging,
piled in a garbage bin.

Three colors you took,
triaged wrinkly wilted
from terminally tinged,
stood still-elegant stems
in half-filled vases to imbibe,
recall their lovely selves,

and every one undrooped,
corollas corpulent with petals
not freshly complexioned
and faintly malodorous
yet beauty if not in bloom
in animate desire.

Raw Tuna and Roses

In memory of Pedro Cuperman

As the chef from Puebla
served our tuna sushi,
my sympathetic chin
perched on a palm

just washed for lunch,
you clinically analyzed
your complicated ex,
Freudian your analysis

of why she dumped you,
her unconscious a net
ever cast to fish pain.
But I write to confess

my attention undivided
to digest your trauma
was halved by a rose
aroma transporting me

to a Mexican woman,
her flesh rose-scented,
her sex like raw tuna,
and when I bit sushi

I truly felt your loss,
my woman gone too
in a whiff of my hand,
rose-scented from soap.

Reflections in Stalled Traffic

in memory of David Ignatow

Upright tombstone dominoes topple
shadows of slabs over a sunset lawn
and so remind us of the physical law:
a body at rest tends to remain at rest.

That's why the dead belong far below
the table of elements, and cemeteries
best are seen distant from highways,
where bodies tend to remain in motion.

Cockroach on the White Shag Rug

Frozen it measures
my superior hulk,
unimpressed by my assumed
dominion over creation, I
no match for its threat:
glazed wing armor,
fine lashing antennae,
bent legs like hairs,
making my own stand on end.

Life knowing its kind,
eons ago it decrypted
my cold wind stare,
my glacial intentions
echoing across the Yukon rug
ingeniously charted
for a zigzag escape.

Long Island Sound

Wafting in weird December warmth,
helicopters rhythmically reiterate

their mission to abort mosquitoes
unseasonably committing manslaughter.

Sunless dawn, dark peace, polluted air
that whirling blades tastelessly season,

outpour of ghost chemicals I visualize,
making reluctant my rise at daybreak.

But I inhale my day, get up to my time
so technologically advanced, hot coffee

sipped to tablet headlines: "West Nile
threatens humans with weak defenses."

"Parents bury teenage football player,"
defenseless against a mosquito heart.

William Shakespeare at the Java Bar

"Regular?" the barista asked,
her volume humbling.

In smart, midtown silence,
before cappuccino eyes,
double-latte eyes, macchiatto eyes,
triple espresso eyes,
forward floated the cup
that deconstructed me:
simply brewed black,
indiscriminate of origin.

Unforgiven, I forgive myself
for ordering so plain
just to rent a chair
and read *Harper's* cover debate
on English's undisputed Champ:
a richly roasted Earl
or a regular Joe?

Ode

Long had we roamed the Upper East Side,
browsing galleries, windows, shops,
scaling the peaks of exquisite art
crafted to seek a human counterpart:
Chinese armies on checkerboard onyx,
geometric designs by primal psyches,
Pointillist trees, Impressionist traffic,
Cubist mammals of chrome bumper parts,
black-and-white slices of time's frozen river
uniquely cropped in camera shots.

But artifice paled before a huge white conch
like none tripped over on public beaches,
marvel if not the great half shell
on which Venus was born a grown woman;
nature's art priceless as the 6 p.m. sun's
bloody descent in a Sophoclean finish,
now hefty bucks in a rose-tinted cube.
Hand in hand we walk on, as my ear,
still flat against shell, hears this roar:
beauty is money, money beauty. That's all
you know on earth, all you've ever known.

2. Portraits in Blues

David Koresh among the Angels

After the fires in Waco, Texas

Unshaven for his memorable death,
through smoked glasses he saw
his bearded father fluorescent
seconds before, faster than flame,
out the bullet hole in his head
he flung his boomerang soul
to one day return with perfect vision,
celestial his tight blue jeans,
and twanging a New Testament rock
at the exact wattage to raise
the dead in the stadium of the world.

Another messiah dying to advertise
his product like a divine detergent:
white, whiter, all the way to bright,
backed by plumed beings radiant too.
But how did David erect such belief
lacking the olden special effects
of when the kingdom of this world
glittered with a film of wonder
and nights blazed planetary signs
magicians divined in the East,
or gathered on the side of a hill,
multitudes inhaled a miracle?

Now that a fatherless boy can just claim
an angel placenta sang in his sleep
umbilical lyrics from eternity,
we must protect that touched child
before he picks up a guitar
and amplifies his prophesies
to questing, dangerous souls—
because we must suspect them all:
Who were those flammable followers,
and what good light did they seek
in the glow of a smoldering man?

My Lost Duchess

At the Bada Bing

Yeah, I shot this, my lost Duchess tanning on—
What beach, Frankie?—that's it, Malibu.
That smile an opening-night marquee
to *mangia* breasts, those longest legs,
highways to heaven that God handmade
for her Hollywood premiere! Did *I* hear?
I heard *Gats*. Last I knows this studio big
cast her as the slut she could play perfect.
What? His Porsche blown up in a ravine?
Marone if life don't twist you like a broad:
swears she loves you but has other plans!
Totaled too's that fine sweet thing's career;
her little heart must mourn in smithereens.
But watch, that delectable bod'll show up,
hot to jerk off whatever telescopic lens.
For her we hit L.A., for her I cashed in debts,
convinced that suntanned *medigan* to try her out.
He did, and she became a full-time actress.
Her dream come true, I flew back home to Jersey.
Hey, you got it wrong. Nobody dumped me
to spread her legs for Mister Casting Couch.
In the sky I saw her shine and said, "Addio."
A couple times she called, but my life's busy.
My business isn't just disposing garbage.
Construction too, with my brother Rocco,
and pole-dancing my new *gumar*, who now
strips just for me, the man she knows I am.

Here. Feast your *malocchio* on that rack.
OK, you're not down here for an estimate
on picking up police department refuse, so?
Whoa! What's this you're telling me? Frankie,
you'da told me if you'd heard this tragedy.
Last week my girl points to the screen, those
teeth I paid for not just blinding the world,
laughing at it, really, on HD prime-time TV,
arm in arm with our dearly departed director.
Who that lives and breathes could pull the plug
on that unbelievable smile I shot in Malibu?
The gun found in that guy's totaled car? See,
life's not fair. Right, Frankie? A shot in the dark.

On the Checkout Line,
Saturday Night Video Rental,
XXX—Adults Only, 1975

Hook his rigid left hand,
in his right a cassette
sleeve absorbs him:
blond the busty embassy
highest ambassadors
of two sexual potentates
undiplomatically visit
front and rear.

That choice third, two under
his right-angle left arm,
company to penetrate
to a new day's solitude,
his right-handed cane
helped his stiff left side
shuffle to this line
just before I joined it
not able to avert
his immersion in that sleeve,
or resist imagining
the moment of that selection,
as privately I screened
the video of his fantasy:

In his packed mansion brain,
perfect bodies perform,
a cassette-scenes orgy,
his perfect among them,
not limbs that now pay
for all the pleasure to come
on this night thanks
to his good right hand.

Call of the Wild

Out a cigar smoker's white Jaguar,
a long-haired fortyish puma,
slender in gray body glove,
paces across the market's lot
to prey on a cart she feeds
the growling automatic door.

I lose her to Produce's jungle.
At Dairy again our paths cross.
Already on line, she swivels:
"Is that my cart or did someone
take it?" Smiling, I offer mine.
Her hand grabs, then declines.

Can a cart's metal conduct
most secret musk thoughts?
Cash transaction, her gait
knows its natural habitat.
I wait for the young cashier
to recover, ring up my milk.

Subway Crustacean

Rag-stuffed shopping bags
furnish the space
his body constructs
of rancid sweat,
grease-clumped hair,
black crescent fingernails,
grime shackles on bare ankles.

You are unwelcome
to his living room,
its transparent walls
the hardened gaze
of your disgust,
in whose solitude
days flow on days,
swamping as smell,
his calendar of urine.

Against his armor
your sight flattens,
slimes downward,
interrogates the floor—
Who are you? What happened—
as he, ball turret loner,
swivels by degrees
his repellent circumference.

Subway Musician

Ma, do I have to?
Yes, till you get it right.

Open the worn case,
remove the violin,
tuck it under chin

as the subway pulls
out of Queens Plaza,
Mozart a passenger,

his magical overture
a train car applauds:
not Mom's wince

but burnished notes
coined pile
the felt lining.

Miss Subways

Seat space for
white girl butts,
and when I sit
don't fail 'tween
some little white guy
and a scrawny Hindu.
Ain't no obese,
just big-boned.

I take good aim.
They gulp spit.
Hips first, I bunch
my coat in front,
then snuuuuuuuugle in,
as they two worm
sideways in respect
for my big, round,
coming-down behind.

Poetry DJ

Okay, crew, a REAL poet
just bopped into your face
'cause that Milton Man is KING,
so another round for Johhhnnnny MMMMMM!
Now don't forget next week
that Raven' Bronx whole pint,
whose name's half P-O-E-try,
flashes his tin-tin-a-bulation
nose to nose with Emmy D.
That's right, a polysyllabic slam!
Frenchified metered madness
and WASP incisor consonants!
So come alone or enjambed, then smoke
your own poems in the open mike.
Next up, the word Zen master,
the word construction worker,
the verbal mojo most quoted
so Bartlett's won't look anorexic,
that iambic pentajazzmeter,
whose mama was a sonnet
and whose papa kept a muse.
Pound those palms and show your ghost for
WILLIE SHAKE-IT-SPEARE!!!!!

Top-Down Corvette Convertible

Fifty years he waited for this
VARRROOOM turbo engine
hoarse as he slows down
sweet before outdoor cafes,
looking to drive fine foxes
Hollywood round the block.

This is heaven, Kingdom come,
painting a Sunday afternoon's lips
with this hot, blood-red stick,
ready for bygone summer girls
to hop in as he had dreamed,
in twos, in threes, for fun, forever.

Like a Lawyer

So you want to know
how *you* can acquire
this pinstripe burnish,
tailored suit, Italian shoes,
gold ring, gold watch,
fine brown attaché,
this convincing pose, hand
sweeping in summation,
and especially a keen
needle meter to detect
those friendly questions
more appropriate
in camera and
not *pro bono*?
Call me. Here's my card.

3. Cosmic Debates

Cosmic Debate

The astronaut said to the cosmonaut:
What points I see I plot
from Earth to Moon to Mars,
out to the farthest star.

The cosmonaut said to the astronaut:
No star is anywhere to say
it's there. Drift timeless,
imagine speed. Call that rocketry.

The astronaut said to the cosmonaut:
All propulsion's to a place,
riding solar winds,
real movement, real soar.

The cosmonaut said to the astronaut:
Ah, to eternal pointlessness
packed ships deliver
the gadgetry of your illusion.

The astronaut said to the cosmonaut:
Look, Earth shrinks behind me!
Connecting coordinates,
I call my dance distance.

The cosmonaut said to the astronaut:
Odysseus in a blank map,
how long will a port
propel you to believe?

Driving to the Beyond: New York Edition

Maybe one departs in late city traffic
a long, break-light bleeding on Seventh,
past armor eyelids over store windows,
parked trailer trucks in elephant sleep
and high-hemmed hookers' sexual gaits
now no attraction to a dead-tired driver
passing red lights to an endless escape
not unlike crossing into New Jersey.

Or maybe no traffic, the avenue a roll,
foot off gas in divine cruise control,
the sky a stadium dark blue to capacity.
Bright neon scripts cry out sad poems
as black breezes blow jazz-salsa-rock
performing in air not intended for you
who'll never again hang a left on Canal
or U-turn avoid the Holland's deep throat,
at whose open mouth greets a grim traffic cop
whose walkie-talkie amplifies dead air.

Maybe your car's wax job instantly dulls,
its bright color fades, its model boxes,
sparkling carets of receding skyline
shrink to dim in your rearview memory
as drops fall from the tip of your nose,
never expecting you'd mourn for yourself,
dead as if broke in expensive Manhattan.

And maybe at the tunnel's flourescent end,
as angel agents waive one-way tolls,
to westbound trucks honking to applaud
an afterlife found so close to the city
you finally glimpse your eternal reward:
no-tab meals at free-parking diners,
any room at mirrored-ceiling motels
where infinite love with one you just met
makes you forget the loss that turns on
windshield wipers that wipe off
every earthly thought but to forgive
everything, even New Jersey's worst drivers,
as you enter the Garden State of Forgiveness.

Shopping Mall

Here in glass combs,
humans swarm,
laden with credit,
buzzing with wants.

Here skinny mannequins
fashionably shame
bulging bodies,
kaleidoscopic vanity.

Here hungry families
converse round pizzas.
Mozzarella words
sag from their lips.

Here wafts the muse
Hot Buttered Popcorn,
come to her multiplex,
eight giant screens.

Here young virtualize
warfare and deaths,
digitized destruction
in cool Game Rooms.

All malls one mall,
London, Mexico, Beijing,
hives for collecting
honey called money.

Strong Wind

after Katrina

Amerikas, Indio told the metal man,
finger toward dark thunder,
his land you violate, his one eye
domes the Caribbean, the House
of Huracán, angry as Edward's God
when out of hibernation he re-forms
in multiple furious gestations.

Where science ends myth knows
why a god must humble mortals
to float on roofs for starving days,
in wet hollows of wrecked hulls
past warped trailers, gutted trucks
nameless, water-swollen limbs,
waterlogged photo memories,
official certificates melted to pulp
as life the river flows in reverse,
time ticking backward to nothingness.

Where science doubts myth knows,
not measurable winds but Huracán's
boundless torrential unhappiness
tore away New Orleans' attics,
drowned trumpets whose song
always soothed anxious Amerikas
but not unappeasable Huracán,

who every summer must reclaim
dominion over his hemisphere,
punish every saint as sinner
so we remember who, above all, rules.

Unlikely Being (1985)

Halley's arrival, its endless parabolic pursuit
of an unreachable
point of departure,
blazing down an infinite fuse that ignites,

from remote timelessness, the finite fuse
of our presence,
marking for us
days on this earth, another seventy-five years

since last seen disappearing to this visibility,
carrying its always
mixed message
plumed by this luminous cosmic quetzal

streaking across the immeasurable black,
exquisite sign
of our extinguishing,
unlikely being it will be we the next time

Night Flight

Up here where nothingness
paints small windows black,
a gray wool of engine roar
blankets shadow passengers

eyes shut in cushioned trust
this simple constellation,
cross of span and fuselage,
does traverse coordinates,

latticed latitudes, longitudes,
blinking across the screen
of an air controller's faith
that out in dark radar miles

a cruising plane will descend
turbulent altitude stairs,
its cabin of rhythmic hearts
mill still weaving a tether

ascendent since San Juan,
arcing toward night glitter
of New York's radio belief
in us now absent, aloft in sleep.

The Glory of the Coming

On the last night of the world,
no commercial interruptions,
the complete, uncut report:
The Tragic Story of Time.

On the last night of the world,
lovers publicly disrobe,
anywhere rhythmically secrete
their last body song.

On the last night of the world,
patients without doctors
pitifully administer
last injections against pain.

On the last night of the world,
for mansion miles
unbroken windows display
valueless treasures.

On the last night of the world,
messiahs suddenly in season
multiply lighted paths
doomed followers follow.

Poem

Make it a cat,
inspiration bones,
each line a leap
of subtlest pause.

Make song its purr,
ambiguity eyes,
its sudden bristle
lustrous metaphor.

Make it to stray,
indebted to none,
lick every heart
as if it were yours.

4. Magisterial Hauntings

Speeding to Teach a Class on Time

NORMAL TRAFFIC
CONDITIONS AHEAD

—a digital highway sign

In dark highway rain
a center-lane hearse,
respectfully conducts,
eroding my time.

Press pedal, change lanes,
traffic rigor mortis,
worn wipers painting
a pointillist scene:

red-dotted parallel lines
swerving toward
what destiny ahead,
a flat, a flood, an accident.

Just as I curse starting late,
motion paints over
windshield colors,
commits me to speed

only to brake, tailgated,
plunged in beam:
the rearview, all-whites
eyes of the hearse.

Class Clown

Red rubber-ball nose,
baguette, cap-bang shoes,
from his open textbook
winged words flutter
over heads of students'
uncontrollable guffaws.

"Follow the great poet's
inspirational flight," he swoons
so steeped, so unaware
up and down desk rows
students' eyes pursue
a dwarf's farting motorbike.

"Who identifies with him?
Raise hands who do."
Ambiguity rules. "Can't he be
everyone—me, you?"
Class rolls in stitches:
"He," the dwarf?

More poems he assigns
decibels too far below
the student conga line
farting as it follows
the rhythmic little rider
out the classroom—

Four-walled solitude
inhaled in one breath
as he plucks his nose,
puts on human shoes,
steps, trips over nothing,
to the laughter of our time.

Teaching Humanities to the Dead

A Magisterial Nightmare

Ambitious skeletons
registered to recover
ancient flesh heritage
resist being transported
to Sophocles' Greece,
destination beyond range
of their cell phones.

"Civilization" and "myth"
launch a hand that lops off
its stumped owner indicting
my use of "hard" words.
Definitions appease. "Now,
how did you like *Oedipus?*"

Popped eyes ricochet,
then a low kitten purr
ascends to a cat's wail
as a rib cage stands,
points articulate bones:
"Who do you think you are
to make us feel dumb?"
Yeah and yeah and yeah
applaud his loud exit,
detonating the door.

I urge them to ponder:
"You who resurrected
from death's monotone
for this second chance
to know how human feels,
Sophocles can show—"

Then every neck cracks,
every socket celebrates
the door swung open:
their classmate Knight
squired by the Dean.

Regaled in deads' cheer,
a guttural, jubilant oink,
Hero instructs his Dean,
lipless teeth in politic grin:
"Sing so all can hear,
our right to be taught
nothing we do not know."

Student D.

Her raised hand a fruit
blossomed from a branch
connected to a trunk
of unschooled ancestors,
they who fed her hunger
of twisted-mile guts
but not enough words.

In one wrong answer
Great Grandpa now free
works at his new job,
hauling wood boards,
sometimes aligning bricks—
good green Negro pay
for empty-milk cries,
hooch for man's nights—
to come home desiring

at the price of an embryo,
a boy come out kicking,
goddamned, sucking for
every necessary thing
to be fed what there was,
mainly manhood words
to recite to a woman,
who'd conjure his own child,

a girl her flesh more work,
more hustle to replace
money's fisted absence,
with no room to dream if
one's parents can't pay,
so if she wanted college,
then go out and borrow,
don't miss a single day,
sit alert in the first row,

tread tides of sentences,
nearly drown in words
a lineage never spoke,
words for white people,
and she *tries*, looks up
definitions, cotton candy
dissolving in her breath,
in the mouth of this effort,
this devouring English class.

Woman Professor of English

Though no man can see my veil,
I am married to scholarly research,
restoring to my gender so maligned
its rightful place since we know time.

Henceforth assumptions about my sex
fry like slavery laws in truth's oil;
men whose eyes beg of my breasts
a mother's mammary subservience

blind will go before they see them.
Let no male think he can enjoin
this independent agent and verb
like some subordinated clause.

Secret Search Committee Memo
(Let's Hire a Real American)

At last we found him, true defiance,
shine in a haystack of applicants.
Profound, if not prototypically,
not one to cave correct politically,
anchored in conviction so refined,
reminding how Academe declined
ever since *objective* lost its tooth
to cut real meaning beside *truth.*

Magisterially cast in tradition,
no publisher of trendy erudition
on races dysfunctional by fate,
on women's high-pitched debate,
the true Story of our provenance
redacted to stop making sense.
This candidate works to disinter
our lost memory of who we were.

Illiterate on what he disrespects,
his indescribable aplomb deflects
questions meant to muck his head,
"Not one minority you've read?"
Stealth fails to describe his gift
of riposte, leveled without shift,
brushing off any need to know
by just shrugging shoulders so.

Tall blond this American dawn
alighted to de-weed our lawn
of rampant Culture War inanities
serially strangling the Humanities.
For him gender, race, and such
"Mankind" capsuled pretty much,
truth whose rays were universal
before Martin Luther King, *et. al.*

Of course, in our conflicted school,
any tenured setting for this jewel
must appease colleagues liberal,
so make him out the multicultural,
cite his citations of Georges Sand,
Ralph Ellison, The Qur'an, and
Don Quixote—quartet he humbles.
After that African who mumbles

so-called scholarship that's rot,
two feminists, a male queer, not
to mention that mañana A.B.D.
who will never finish his degree,
now diversité c'est whom we say,
a once normal curriculum vitae,
espousing plain, unconciliatory,
American Truth, American Story.

5. Anytown Child

Sweety

Old friends passed away
made this neighborhood home.
Now she bemoaned decline:
ninety-nine-cent stores, fast foods,
people who lacked time
for pleasant chats over tea
because at seventy she craved
pretty pastry on an afternoon.

Our hallway sounds always opened
the door to her kindness,
generous hands welcoming,
"Sweety," what she called Kiki,
who gave her that name,
young guest not yet three
invited to converse
over cookies and milk.

When her door became deaf,
Kiki was told Sweety slept,
one white lie to keep
a neighbor's privacy.
But truth craved a sweeter story.
"Yes, she's happy in heaven,"
we assured, praying that Sweety
found her friends over tea,
fresh again, pretty as pastry.

Jury Duty

They fill the court's corridor benches,
sons awaiting trials with mothers
whose eyes, murky with old pain,
don't bother with who passes.

Their sons are lanky, some look up,
glances that hang out, stab you,
and even that seems like a bore.
You strain not to judge by looks.

On a mother's lap a baby sleeps,
its face under her gentle hand;
one mother lifts a cardboard cup,
another's hands hold each other.

Every mother prays the judge
reads the riddle in her son's heart,
deciphers good from confusion,
she a victim in his every crime

here to defend her bad good boy,
the splintery cross on her back,
up the steep hill, and then down,
and then up again, broken back.

Unwrapped Present

Her ultimate dolly,
chubby replica limbs,

warm leavened chest,
bud lips, mouth yawning

a lower case o,
precise its wail

and perfect its sleep
exactly as she prayed,

a wisp-haired head
on a heartbeat pillow.

International Relations

Islamic Iran's crescent sword
beheaded the Peacock Throne,
so overseas colonels went home,
Sharaam in step with his father.

Then the Yen karate-kicked
little Jennifer's family's trust
in all save God and a house
miles out on Long Island,

and when the dollar bounced back,
Panasonic's new plans recalled
another blue suit to Kyoto,
from where Chohiro once wrote.

Now you stare up at windows
between tossing upward a ball,
high cupped hands welcoming
one friend that returns.

In Memoriam

(for Eliza Izquierdo, 1989–1995)

Everyone wanted a monument to battered children:
parents who promised never to hit theirs again,
parents who knew of children who suffer,
siblings who buried a corpse they'll forget,
grandparents who didn't live long enough,
neighbors who knew they could have helped,
mayors who cannot take time out to play,
governors whose budgets don't include toys,
presidents who never read us bedtime stories,
the planet at war over where to place the monument.

Anytown Child

"My daughter is a downtown child . . ."
　　　—a Manhattanite

Kiki interrupts my thoughts,
'Cause your cozy, she swoons,
forgetting by now
that midtown waiter's scowl

at having to join tables, lose
a bigger tab to an ungrown,
halved his calculated tip,
spoiling adult atmosphere.

Like me childless years ago,
a life I habitually review,
finding in no Manhattan chat
no plumbing as profound

as from this literary critic,
pristine genius engrossed
in tenderest resolutions,
Little House on the Prairie.

Bedtime hug for my hug,
my mind transported visiting
an acquaintance's little boy
hospitalized after a truck

mangled his bike and skull,
comatose sophistication
occupying an adult table
under a waiter's scowl.

6. Poems of the Freak

Poems of the Freak

Editor's Prologue

Only his mother ever saw his face,
Or knew his name until she died.
No relatives, photographs survive
To piece the jagged fragments.
Journalists and social scientists,
Scoping post-mortem mystery,
Focused on his novelty denied
The world attracted to anomaly,
Flesh only legend till we knew
This lean, lasting body of poetry.

For years, omniscient rumor
Spread amorphously without pity
A cruel, animated portrait:
Armless hands like whale's fins
Or the single mitten-like limb
Branching from his scaled back,
Head ballooning on some days,
Other days aged and shriveled,
The mouth a rose on his cheek.

From this new womb his poems
In words adult since childhood,
Contour kept from us now visible
Returns righted from the bosom
Of death reliever of his sorrows
One day, particulars unknown
Except for the lore of a bonfire
His mother erected to forge him
Formless in "God's black sight."

I.
Mirrors

My mother forbids them
but bathes me
in my wet reflection.

I try to piece my face,
but she shatters it,
points to her eyes,

"See yourself here."
But nothing reflects
on her trembling lids.

2.
Only on Some Nights

My door the womb
my soul presses against,
kicking to be, opens
only on some nights.

Holding my one hand
fingered like hers,
night holding the other,
my mother leads me.

Upward dive my eyes
into black-water sky,
far my heart swims
across a lake of stars.

I want to be alive
every single night.
"Not in full moons."
Drooling, I mouth "Why?"

3.
Moon Beauty

A freak's head changing
round to thin to shame,

face from whose pocks
distance mines beauty.

How far must I be
to be seen beautiful?

4.
Shadow Side

In my crater mouth,
every possible utterance
awaits its turn
never to be said.

5.
All One

Of my poems etched
with fisted pencil,
always facedown,
my unheard heart
hammering the floor
I never cremate
coherent ones, the lies.

Only mirrors of me,
truth composed
of gibberish
like "grubpiclok"
and "kmopeinoque,"
word freaks
I crumple,
joyfully torch.

6.
Meop

Some nights the bulb's light
inflicts pain,
my feet balloon,
sores erode my elbows,
sounds hatch on my lips
only to die and rot,
my pencil will not write
because I remember
who is pushing it, I,
humpbacked, pimply-skinned.

Then, poet of spit,
I splatter out growls,
break not lines but chairs,
overturn my mattress
while upstairs my mother
recites holy words.

7.
The Night

Another kind of mother,
she ages us in her belly
except in this birth
we are not expelled
but sucked deeper into
her wide black pupil
that only sees
us invisible.

8.

Father

Before answering my written question, she exhales.
"He's around you, like the moonlight."
I meant my real father, maker of freaks.
"He was handsome outside, like you inside."
She explains different kinds of seeing.

She once erupted, "Just like your father!"
I, just a boy, persisted at something.
She swears she meant the Father of all things.
"One morning he was gone," once breezed
through a crack in the wall and forever
in my ears. Who is my father? I still ask,
always imagining a handsome man.

9.
Incandescence

When the book yawns,
I erase light,
become absence,
blank memory,

my overfed eyes
vomit into dark
the black ink
of what I read.

I pray for fever,
a whale's breath,
the swallowing
of God's black sight.

Title Index

I

First Line Index

www.ingramcontent.com/pod-product-compliance
Lightning Source LLC
Chambersburg PA
CBHW010857090426
42737CB00020B/3408